Secrets to an
Exceptional
Job Interview

Secrets to an Exceptional Job Interview

By Karen Durand

POWER LINES

About the Author

Karen Durand is a brand and shopper marketing executive, retired, with 32 years of business experience which included the following positions: Senior Manager, Shopper Marketing Center of Excellence at Kimberly-Clark, Corp, Vice President Marketing, Specialty Foods Group, Inc.; Group Manager, Business Development at International Paper; Director of Marketing and Director of Corporate Communications and Investor Relations at Gibson Greetings and she consulted for a variety of other Consumer Product Goods (CPG) & Business to Business (B2B) companies.

She is currently a community college workshop instructor and mentor on topics such as how to find your dream job, how to write an effective resume, how to start and grow a business, how to write a business plan and develop marketing strategies and campaigns that work, as well as how to design an effective marketing plan mix, which includes traditional and online marketing tactics to grow sales. She has worked with and coached hundreds of clients and students to ensure they either successfully find the job of their dreams or start and grow their own business.

TABLE OF CONTENTS

Introduction

Looking for a job is like a roller coaster ride, with high--highs, such as when you get the call for an interview or the job offer, and low-lows, when the rejection letter arrives or there is no response after 3 tries. But at the end of the search, getting the job you want makes it all worthwhile.

Yes, there will always be someone who has more experience, or something MORE than you have. In fact, when teaching, I hear time and time again from my students, "I don't have enough experience," "I don't have the right education," "I've been out of the work force for so long, no one will ever hire me." However, after working with many job candidates I've found that is simply NOT TRUE!

There IS a "right job" for everyone and your resume, cover letter, and follow up thank you letters are critically important first steps on the road to success, because they represent YOU before you ever talk to anyone. In fact, they are often the reason you even get a foot in the door in the first place. Then once you get the call, your preparation, sheer presence, and interviewing skills will close the deal.

First, you need to understand that an Employer only cares about one thing... How well the job is going to be done!

Therefore, your job is twofold:

- To convince an employer that you have what it takes to be successful in this new position or career.
- To establish yourself as a professional person with high standards and excellent writing skills showcased through a great resume, cover letter, and thank you letter so you are one of a handful of candidates who are invited in the door for an interview.

Even with very little job experience you can get a job. Great preparation in the following 5 areas is the key:

1. Understand the Landscape
2. Writing an Effective Resume
3. Designing a Great Cover Letter
4. Preparing and Sending a Thank You Letter
5. Preparation & Practice for the Interview

UNDERSTAND THE LANDSCAPE

01

Actions to Complete Before Writing a Resume

The first step is to take a few minutes to thoroughly assess your interests, accomplishments, job targets and skills which you will use as a resume' foundation and then conduct some marketing research so you have a thorough understanding of the marketplace. This includes:

- Identify and list your:

  - □ **Hard Skills** which are skills earned through work experience and education, i.e. computer expertise, medical training, certifications and higher-level education completed, etc.

  - □ **Soft Skills**, which are descriptive of your personality and work ethic, i.e. organizational ability, goal oriented, punctuality, problem solving ability, etc. *Hint: Ask a coach or mentor their thoughts on how they would describe you.*

As you complete this exercise start to think about and write down situational examples where you have demonstrated your Hard and Soft Skills in previous jobs or volunteer situations, even if they were in a different field. For ex. If 'compassion patient care' or 'timeliness' are soft skill attributes outlined in a job description, you probably have an example where you've demonstrated these behaviors in past work or volunteer situations.

The key to writing an effective resume is to showcase your skills through examples of past behavior which will be discussed in more detail under the Resume Writing portion of this book.

- **Conduct Primary and Secondary Marketing Research to Gather Marketplace Data**

  □ **Secondary research** includes researching key job targets on line, ex. job boards, industry specific sites and company sites you are targeting in order to get a clear idea of what Hard and Soft skills are being requested in each job description.
  You will also use this secondary information to survey your professional environment in order to understand jobs available, trends and areas of growth in your industry, and to ensure you have the competencies required for success and know what the hot topics are in your field. Secondary research sources may include:
  - Job boards and listings, ex. Indeed.com is an aggregate job board
  - Library, i.e. Trade Journals, database subscriptions

- Online Industry Periodicals, ex. smartbriefs.com are Free Newsletters which aggregate all industry information and send it to your email
- Company websites, i.e. About Us, Press Releases, Management Profiles, Annual Reports, Career Openings, Reviews and Testimonials pages
- Google Online Media by using key words and phrases, including company name, industry and job types, etc.
- Key word searches/alerts set on your computer, ex. Google news, Keotag, Addictomatic, LinkedIn, Twitter, etc.
- 3rd Party sites, ex. Glass door for salary and cultural type information
- Discussions with experts or people who work in the field or for a specific company, i.e. see Informational Interview section below.
- Observation of employees on site as a customer or vendor

☐ ***Why Is Secondary Research Important?*** Knowledge is power. This information will allow you to define how and where you want to work, ex. customer (retail) versus business facing; provide organization size and culture information; industry segmentation and geographic locations and possibly identify new career opportunities which have been created because of industry changes. It also allows you to assess what is needed to keep your skill set competitive.

☐ Primary Research, or Informational Interviews is also an important tactic to utilize

- Your job search process is a great time to ask family and friends for assistance. What this involves is asking for help from individuals in your life who can assist you in finding a job. This includes most family members, friends, neighbors, colleagues, and professional acquaintances. The more the better, because the chances are really good that someone knows someone who knows someone in the field you are going to work in. *Why is this critically important? Because most jobs are obtained through a networking contact.*

  Most people want to help. The key to using this tactic effectively is that you are NOT asking anyone to hire you. Rather you are looking for information and identifying people who may be willing to talk to you about their experience in this field, including information about specific companies they have worked for and about the industry itself. *(Hint: this is an effective networking tactic since an added benefit is that it gives you an opportunity to talk about your skills and interests, if asked and increases awareness of your job search)*

  o <u>Conversational Approach:</u> When someone asks," Hi, how's it going", be ready to say, "Great, I'm completing my degree/or recently completed a degree in x and looking for new job in x field, <u>who</u> do you know or can recommend I talk to which may be able to give me some insight into x field. *(Note: Do NOT say "<u>do</u> you know anyone who I can talk to...", because that gives them an automatic opportunity to say 'no.' Even if they cannot remember anyone at the moment you ask, they will think about it and respond when you email a thank you note to them.)*

- o <u>Written Approach:</u> Since we do not actually see many of the people we know in person very often, an E-mail networking cover letter is an effective way to reach each of your contacts. It should include the reason you are writing and the ask for help, ex. 'recently graduated or graduating soon with x degree and would like to understand more about this field/your company, etc. *(Important: Do NOT ask for a job).* Who do you know that may be good for me to talk to. Or, if it's the potential interview contact, say, 'x referred me to you..." Then ask if they are willing to meet with you for coffee or talk by phone to share their expertise about this field. *Remember to send a thank you note after these interactions as well.*

- ☐ **Preparation** Regardless of the approach, before an actual Informational Interview prepare a list of questions ahead of time to ask by phone or in person. This will allow both of you to relax. Be clear that you are not asking for a job, but rather would like to discuss their knowledge of the industry and benefit from their expert advice. Be sincere and upfront about asking for their advice. Appendix 1 includes a list of networking questions you can ask. Below is an example of the networking process:

  - • "Thank you for meeting/talking to me. As I mentioned I recently graduated/or will be graduating soon with an x degree and would like to understand more about this field/your company."

- "What has been your experience in this field / company?" Follow up with questions regarding their likes/dislikes, biggest challenges
- Ask a question or two about what you found from your secondary research to get their perspective.
- "What would you recommend to someone like me, with some/limited experience in this field? Any watch outs I should be aware of?"
- End by asking **_who else_** they think you should talk to who might be willing to share their knowledge and if you can mention them as the referral.
- Be sure to get their contact information for follow up.

☐ **After the Information Interview or Networking Contact:** Whether it's on the phone, email or in person, ALWAYS follow up with email Thank You note within 24 hours after the meeting or call. Make it <u>brief</u>, but to the point. See Appendix 2 for Thank You Letter examples. Below is an example of the thank you note structure:

- Thank them for their time, it was very helpful... (include a specific point or two from your conversation). Don't be afraid to show the enthusiasm you feel about launching your professional career
- Add one sentence which reinforces that you are skilled, qualified, employable person with a lot to offer and their advice will be a great help in positioning yourself to be successful in this field

- Thank them for a referral/or for letting you know when they think of anyone else who you may benefit in talking to.
- Include your contact information (telephone and email) in your salutation, but NOT your resume, unless requested, in case they want to forward your email to a hiring colleague.

☐ Remember: You are NOT asking for a job, however, this technique, while scary to start, is very effective in increasing your network size and chances of getting a job. Since most jobs are procured through networking, this is a great method of creating your own network within your chosen field.

☐ ***Why Informational Interviews?*** The more people who know about you and what you want and need, the greater the results. You will find when asked most people are flattered and willing to talk about themselves and are willing to help, if you're not specifically asking them for work and if they do not see you as a competitor or threat. This technique allows them to remember you and refer you if they sense genuine interest and competence from you.

Informational Interviews are an effective technique you can engage in throughout your job search and actually through your entire career. Create a master list of the names of everyone and keep track of contacts and results. Once you get a job consider going back and letting your initial referral know the outcome and provide another Thank You for their help.

WRITING AN EFFECTIVE RESUME

02

Your Resume is your critically important first impression with prospective employers!

However, when writing this document, it is important to remember that it's NOT about you.

Remember, when hiring, an employer's ONLY concern from their perspective is... How well the job is going to be done. **Write to appeal to them – not yourself!**

You need to demonstrate through your resume that you are an exceptional candidate which meets or exceeds the criteria in the job description. For example, if they are looking for someone who demonstrates 'compassionate patient care' or 'timeliness' as soft skill attributes and a certain education degree (hard skill), as outlined in a job description, your educational accomplishments and some of your past job or volunteer examples better reflect all of this in your resume or you will not get past the first key word scan on the computer.

What Are Employers Looking For?

Given you are on a level playing field with other candidates, i.e. by knowing the field you are applying for and having some education and volunteer or work experience to support employment in that field, employers are looking for the following attributes:

- Employees who can help them succeed
- Honest employees who have integrity and are hard working
- Employees who can problem solve and work independently
- Employees who are reliable, i.e. showing up on time, with infrequent absence and plan to stick around for a while
- Good communication skills – Employees have a good command of the native language spoken at the company and if relevant, a second language
- Employees who have basic computer, math and reading skills

Seems simple right? These are basic skills we assume most people have, correct? You would be surprised how many employers will tell you how difficult it is to find candidates with these attributes. Through your resume, you have the opportunity to shine, and showcase the fact that you DO have these skills and are the right candidate for the job.

What a RESUME really is:

- Your Marketing and Sales tool to Sell Your Product = YOU!
- An introduction to people who will eventually hire you
- The way to establish yourself as a professional person with high standards
- How to showcase your skills accurately and honestly to show you have what it takes to be successful in this new position or career
- A focus on "key words" which reflect what the company or individual who might hire you is looking for and how you can meet their needs *(Hint: look at the desired attributes in the job description).* This last point is important because an employer's first pass through a stack of Resumes is often a "key word" computer screening, followed by a 10-20 second "visual scan" of the cover letter and resume only for those that pass the initial screen.

The key to a truly effective Resume is to include enough information to sell yourself, while leaving them wanting more so they contact you for an interview as a next step.

Types of Resumes

There are different types of resumes and everyone has their own favorite format which they will recommend you use. The key is pick one and stick with it. Two key formats you will hear about most often are the **Functional Resume** format, which focuses on your skills and abilities designed to cover gaps in employment, which is really a non-issue these days since 30 year careers with one company are a thing of the past, and the **Reverse Chronological Resume** format which lists your most recent job listed first in chronological order.

We are going to focus on the Reverse Chronological Resume since it's the most common, is easy to read and preferred by employers.

The elements of an effective Reverse Chronological Resume include the following categories, which we'll go into more detail below.

- Heading – Name, address, phone number
- Objective
- Skills
- Work Experience
- Education
- Volunteer Experiences

Guidelines When Writing A Resume

The easiest way to start is with a simple blank Microsoft Word document. I recommend avoiding the use of Resume templates which can be found online. They do not scan well and are difficult to make changes to. Keep in mind, scannability of key words, content and basic format are more important than looking pretty with borders, colors and boxes. It's also easier to cut and paste into a company's online system, if needed.

Throughout the resume, you want to keep the reader's interest and highlight your accomplishment in a concise and effective way. Try for a functional, direct writing style that focuses on the use of verbs and other words that imply action on your part which characterizes you to a potential employer as an energetic, active person, who completes tasks and achieves results from their work.

Choose words that display your strengths and demonstrate your initiative. Avoid a conversational tone and take Out "My", "Mine", "This", and "I".

Remember: It's NOT about you, it is about what you can do for the employer.

General Rules When Writing Resumes

In most cases, it is safe to assume your resume will be scanned online for review and key word search, therefore it is recommended you use the following format guidelines:

- Use a standard font, i.e. Times New Roman or Calibri and use boldface and capitalization to set off elements, such as your name and section headers.
- Eliminate underlining, italics and fancy scripts, dashes and brackets, as well as boxes and graphics because they do not scan well.
- Place the most important information at the top of the first page and try and keep information and elements at the left margin.

- List each telephone number on its own line in the header.

- Use keywords to ensure your qualifications are picked up.

- Be descriptive in your title, ex. Legal Office Assistant vs. Assistant and do NOT use any acronyms.

- Spell check! Spell check! Spell check! Online systems are not infallible, for example, take an 'a" out of the word 'manager' and you get 'manger' which is still a word.

- Capitalize proper nouns, such as names of schools, colleges, and universities; names of companies; and brand names of products along with major words in the names and titles of books, tests and articles in the body of your resume.

- Use numerals in a resume rather than spell out the number. The exception is academic resumes.

- Never spell out the words "percent" or "dollar" and use the symbol, as in 30% or $12 million for a cleaner look.

- After pasting your resume into an online system go back and fix or eliminate bullet points before hitting 'save' or 'submit.'

- From a punctuation standpoint, use commas to separate words in a series and a semicolon to separate series of words that already include commas within the series.

- Use a colon to show that examples or details follow that will expand or amplify the preceding phrase.

- Use a period to end every sentence OR do not use at all. Just be consistent throughout the document.

- If you use any punctuation in an unusual way in your resume, be consistent in its use and be sure to double check and fix these areas if you cut and paste your resume copy into an online system because they don't translate well.
- When attaching a resume online, try to send as a PDF document so it can not be modified, unless asked for a specific type of file by the employer.
- When in doubt consult a style manual such as Words into Type (Prentice Hall); The Chicago Manual of Style (The University of Chicago Press) and the Microsoft word grammar guide.
- Use a high-quality laser printer and white paper for scannability.

Let's Write Your Next RESUME... Now that you have the basics let's get started: See Appendix 3-7 for sample resume examples of each section below.

Resume Header

This section is at the top of the page. It consists of your name, centered and bolded so it is the first thing a prospective employer sees, followed by your contact information either centered directly below or right and left justified if you have a lot of experience and need additional space within the document due to depth of experience.

- **Your Name** – use your full first and last name. Do not use nicknames. Then bold and increase font size so it stands out at the top of the page.

- **Mailing Address** – include your street address, city, state, zip code. *Note: if it is located out of the employers area because you're moving, you will to include why in your cover letter.*

- **Telephone Number** – include a number that you are going to answer. (area code) xxxxxxx. Be sure to include a short professional sounding voice mail message.

- **Email Address** – make sure it is professional sounding even if you must open a new email account, ex. First.Last name@... A new email account may also help you keep track of all your job search correspondence.

- **Social Media Accounts** – *IMPORTANT:* DO NOT include them, however, I DO recommend you clean up your account history, set accounts on private and unfriend anyone who posts less than professional content before you start your job search since this is one of the first places reviewed and screened by potential employers.

OBJECTIVE

In this section clearly state what you are looking for from a job and career direction. This is particularly important if you are changing careers or finishing a degree. It eliminates uncertainty about the type of job you are applying for as it relates to the job description.

Content should be short and to the point. Stress how you, as the ideal candidate, <u>will benefit the company</u>, and include "key words" which highlight your abilities and achievements specific to the job description:

A/an _____ position in an organization where _____ and _____ would be needed A/an _____ position in an organization seeking _____ and _____

Examples:
- A culinary position with a progressive organization who values a team player able to work in a fast pace environment and who knows the importance of kitchen cleanliness and safe food handling.
- To perform accurate diagnoses, assessment, testing and repairs of technology issues to create robust solutions which meet or exceed customers and employee's needs.
- A cost accounting position with a company who is looking for an individual who is self-motivated, detail oriented, analytical and has a desire to learn and excel.

SKILLS

This section is optional and should be included if you have <u>HARD</u> skills <u>relevant to the job</u> which are difficult to include in your education and work experience sections. Ex. Fluency in a foreign language, extensive travel abroad, knowledge of specific computer applications and certificates or licenses. If you have applied for a license, but not yet received it, you can include the phrase "application pending." Be sure any information listed here is completely accurate as potential employers will fact check.

I DO NOT recommend including <u>SOFT</u> skills in this section, which may include words such as, detail oriented, multitasker, enthusiastic, dependable and highly self-motivated, responsible, reliable, punctual; take pride in work, excellent communication and interpersonal skills; professional customer service, diplomatic, patient with all types of individuals and quick learner. These are your own opinion of yourself!

The best way to demonstrate SOFT skills is through your written examples under the Work Experience section and through your in person professionalism and actions related to the application, interview responses and follow up actions for the position.

Which Goes First?

The next two Resume sections are your **Work Experience** and **Education** and I am often asked which goes first. My answer is, "It depends"

- If you are changing careers with a relevant degree, ex. your past work experience is as a server or manager at a local restaurant, but your new degree or training is for a Ultrasound Technician position, I recommend you list Education first to support both your Objective and to quickly indicate why you are applying for a very different kind of job than your past work history indicates.

- If you have existing job experience in your field, along with the relevant education or training and your goal is to move to a more challenging position, then I recommend that you list your Work Experience section first, followed by the Education section.

Regardless of which you choose, it is important to include key words in both sections related to the job description and qualifications for electronic scanning selection.

EDUCATION & TRAINING

This section is often the deciding factor in an employer's decision to include you on the short list for an interview. It is your greatest asset if your related work experience is minimal. For entry level type positions, employers are looking for employees without a lot of bad habits, who they can train and mold, so vast work experience may not be required.

In general, advanced education shows dedication and advanced critical thinking skills, no matter what the degree is in, so it is recommended that you include either other degrees and certifications completed or other college or training if not completed, but hours completed are significant, even if it is not directly relevant to the field you are applying for. See Appendix 4 and 5 for examples.

In this section you are going to list your educational achievements in <u>reverse chronological date order</u>, i.e. most recent first. If you have college credits, you do not need to list your high school unless you received specialized training, specific to your work field, since college education implies you have completed high school. Information included for each college or university is as follows:

- College or university name, city and state
- Degree title earned, with Month/Year date Graduated or Expected Graduation Date, right justified across from the title on the page.
- Additional Certifications if they relate to the job. For ex. CPR or First Aid in the medical field or computer program expertise in any field.
- Only include your college grade point average if you graduated recently and it is an "A" and list any awards or recognition achieved, ex. Dean's List; Honor Roll, only if it is a recent achievement. See Appendix 4 for an example.

Repeat this information for next most recent education achieved, as needed.

WORK EXPERIENCE

This section includes your Professional Work and any Co-op/Clinical/Intern Experience, which you list in <u>reverse chronological date order</u>, i.e. most recent first. Information included for each job is as follows:

- Company Name, City, State

- Title of position held and Month/Year dates you were employed there, right justified across from position title on the page. *Tip: Leaving off the actual month and day you were hired and left the company helps cover possible timeline gaps.*

- Then 2-4 bullet points which summarize your job experience. <u>This is a critically important section as it mostly likely will be the experience which sets you apart.</u>

- Choose 'action" oriented words, such as, Performed, Promoted to, Managed,

- Presented, Responsible for, Developed, Communicated, Prepared, Designed, Reduced, etc. that display your strengths, accomplishments, promotions and demonstrate your initiative, progressive responsibility and teamwork. And include words describing activities that may relate to the job you're applying for, ex. cleanliness, training, compassionate patient/customer care, record keeping, etc.

- *Tip: Spend the most time here to get it right. The goal is to showcase your hard and soft skills in action as they relate to the job you're applying for.*

Examples showing action and achievements:
- Responsible for customer service, supervising staff and managing inventory
- Experienced in inpatient and outpatient interactions
- Promoted to lead manager of a high volume department, responsible for hiring, payroll, cash control and customer service

Positions held in the military service should also be listed as jobs in this section and treated in the same manner. In fact, military experience is looked on favorably from both a skills and work habits learned standpoint, as well as helping employers meet Equal Employment Opportunity Commission (EEOC) hiring guidelines in the U.S. See examples in Appendix 4 and 5.

If you are changing career paths via education and have the opportunity to showcase Intern or Clinical Experience in the new field, while in school, it is recommended you consider dividing this section into two separate parts to directly showcase relevant work experience in the field first under a separate header as shown in Appendix 3. And it is important to note that clinical and intern experience does count if employers are looking for at least one year experience in the field. Military experience can be integrated in reverse chronological order within either section as it applies to the field you are applying for as shown in the resume examples in Appendix 4 & 5.

Example of Work Experience Resume section headers:

PROFESSIONAL WORK EXPERIENCE

- **CLINICAL (Intern) EXPERIENCE** – list all related job experience to your new field, in reverse chronological date order.
- **WORK EXPERIENCE** – list all non related civilian and military jobs, which may include 'soft skill' experiences you may refer to in an interview later on, in reverse chronological date order.

VOLUNTEER EXPERIENCE

In this last section of the resume include involvement in activities outside of work and school, through organizations and clubs to indicate initiative, dedication, leadership and good social skills.

The exception would be where you might have had a responsible volunteer position for a number of years, in lieu of a paid position. In this case you may want to include this role in your Work Experience as shown in one Appendix 6.

When work experience is light, volunteering or interning in your field of interest often makes a difference and provides examples to use during an interview. See example in Appendix 7. Professional memberships, publications, along with committee and leadership positions in these types of organizations also help if relevant to your job search and indicates you stay up-to-date and connected in your field.

Tips: Only include current or recent information which is relevant to the job search. Limit personal information by excluding volunteer positions related to playing on a team, club memberships, coaching a child's sport as well as membership in politically or socially sensitive groups.

Information Not Included on a Resume but Needed:

REFERENCES AVAILABLE UPON REQUEST – Do <u>NOT</u> include this statement at the bottom of your resume. It is assumed you will have References, which you will need to provide separately, when requested, usually on a Job Application after you have made it through the interview.

Tip: That said, do make a list of your references on a separate piece of paper with accurate contact information, i.e. telephone number, email address and a brief statement listing their relationship to you, ex. High School Football Coach, Band Teacher, Employer, etc. Be sure to ask folks before you add them to the list. It is a great way to inform them that you're looking for a job and ask for their help. Also keep them informed periodically about the status of your search and when they may be receiving a call.

Other information you may need to provide on a Job Application, but NOT on a resume includes personal information: ID's, driver license, passport number, citizenship paper, etc.

DESIGNING A GREAT COVER LETTER

03

Cover Letters are the ASK. Asking effectively is the first key to getting what you want, so you want to standout by clearly indicating what job you are applying for, briefly listing your qualifications, clarifying any puzzling data in your resume, such as an out of state address and an up-coming move and suggest a meeting or follow up time in your final paragraph. Be sure your wording communicates your enthusiasm about the opportunity.

Cover Letters are short. NOT a rehash of your resume!

When writing a cover letter, make sure it is personalized to the specific individual and company you are addressing. Print it on the same quality paper you use for your resume and keep an accurate record of all resumes sent out and results of each mailing.

The Cover Letter should be no longer than 1-3 paragraphs in polite business like language as shown in Appendix 8 and 9 and include:

Your name, address and phone number
Date
Name and address of person and company to whom you are sending your resume

The salutation:
Dear Mr. or Ms. OR To Whom It May Concern

Opening 1-2 sentence paragraph to explain why you are writing
One 1-2 sentence paragraph that outlines why you want to work for the company and briefly what qualifications and experiences you can bring to the position
Final short paragraph closes the letter and invites the reviewer to contact you for an interview. Include phone number and best time to reach you
The closing (Sincerely or Yours truly) followed by your signature with your name typed under it

If you send as an Email Cover Letter it is ideal if the entire letter, 100%, is visible in the browser window. Include a descriptive Subject Line for your e-mail message matching the ad you are applying for and include a formatted (Microsoft Word) resume as an attachment unless the ad you have responded to specifies "no attachments"; in that case, simply cut and paste your resume as text below the salutation. Don't forget to check formatting and run your email program's spell checker before sending.

About one week after you send your cover letter and resume, if you haven't heard anything, contact the potential employer to confirm your resume has arrived and ask whether an interview might be possible. If not, ask when they might be making their decision or next steps, and if it would be alright to follow up around that timeframe. Record the name of people you speak with and any other information you gather.

When calling, treat ALL people you speak with a great deal of respect, including assistants and receptionists who are the gate keepers to the hiring manager and will comment on your behavior.

It is scary to make a cold call, but remember: All they can say is "no". Then you know it is time to move onto the next potential company for employment.

Appendix 8 and 9 include example cover letters for review.

PREPARING AND SENDING A THANK YOU LETTER

04

You can never send too many thank you notes! EVERY-ONE who helps or offers to help you with your job search should receive one since it is common courtesy to thank people who have helped you. This action truly gives you a competitive advantage since it is remembered by the recipient and most job candidates do not complete this step.

In addition to sending one to everyone who interviews you, I also recommend you send one to each networking contact who shares time or advice or contact names with you. Appendix 2 includes Thank You letter examples.

Steps for success when writing Thank You Notes:
- Gather Business Cards or a contact email from everyone you talk to and write a brief note on each to remember them by.
- Try and always send via email **within <u>24 hours</u>** of the meeting or interview. Decision making happens very fast these days. You do not want to miss the window of opportunity.

- Personalize a standard email you may design with at least one point you either learned about that individual or reinforces a point important to them. This is particularly important when you are following up on group or multiple interview situations, because they will compare your Thank You notes with each other.
- Thank them for their valuable time and confirm your interest in the position based on key points discussed, outlining why you are the best candidate for the position or why the field is of interest to you.
- Don't be afraid to show the enthusiasm you feel about launching your professional career.
- Don't handwrite unless you have exceptionally clear handwriting and they are very short notes, and unless you have a method of delivering them within the 24-hour window.

If you don't hear back from the hiring company for a couple of weeks longer than you expected, don't panic. MUCH could be going on that has nothing to do with you at all. However, do reach out by email or phone to see what is happening.

Do NOT contact them daily – or even weekly – for a decision. And, NEVER suspend your job search while you wait for a decision from an employer, even if the job is your dream job.

PREPARING AND PRACTICING FOR THE INTERVIEW

05

Great news! You have received the call for an interview, either on the phone or in person. Now it is all about preparation and practice. Don't panic, whether you are an introvert or extrovert, advanced preparation and practice will ensure your success.

Know that you are one of only a select few, out of hundreds of applicants, who have made the cut for this interview, all based on your hard skills, background and experience portrayed primarily in your cover letter, resume and thank you letter. It is safe to assume that the others you are now competing against for the job have similar skills.

If that is the case, how do employers decide who to hire? Remember their one priority?... their perception of "How well the is job going to be done!"

At this point it's going to be about verifying your hard skills knowledge and most importantly how you interact with the hiring team via your soft skills during the interview. Studies have shown that the hiring decisions are based on 40% Attitude, 25% Appearance, 25% Communication Skills and 10% Job Qualifications of the candidate. Why? As I just stated, if the three candidates invited in for an interview have similar hard skills, then the hiring company is primarily looking for who they want to work with and who will get the job done, as demonstrated through your soft skills.

Pre Interview Preparation is Critical

Below is a list of 8 key actions you should take before the interview.

1. **Review and Update Your Research** – Pull out and review all of the information you have about that company. Revisit online research sites, such as the company website, job boards, GlassDoor.com and industry news sites to refresh your knowledge about the company and industry. Think about and write down some thoughtful questions to ask the interviewer to demonstrate your knowledge and interest.

2. **Know where you're going** – Map out directions to the interview site via your favorite navigation app and allow plenty of time to get there. Plan to arrive 5-15 minutes early to the interview site. If you arrive to your destination even earlier, find a nearby coffee shop or sit in your vehicle and go over your notes one more time.

3. **Get plenty of Sleep the night before, Set Your Alarm and Fuel Up in the Morning** – Be alert, fresh, and at your best on interview day. Set your alarm so you allow plenty of time to get ready. In fact, if you're not a morning person set 2 alarms if

you have an early interview. Also eat something <u>before</u> you get dressed in your interview clothes and leave. You do not want your clothes soiled or your stomach growling if the interview is running long, because it is going well.

4. **Get your paperwork together** – Plan to bring a few extra copies of your resume, a portfolio with a couple of pens and a pad of paper, which includes a few questions you will ask them; a copy of your one page list of references, with contact information and any brief research notes, if needed. If relevant, you may also want to bring a portfolio with some of your work samples for demonstration purposes, if it's not proprietary information. Assemble this in a professional format the night before, along with your bag, notebook and keys, so you are less likely to forget anything important.

5. **Assemble Your Professional Looking Interview Outfit the night before** – Given accepted relaxed business casual attire styles these days, it may be difficult to decide what to wear. A good rule of thumb is to dress at least one level up from what is typically worn in their office day to day. This means, if jeans and polo shirts are the norm, then you wear dress pants with a button down shirt, and maybe a tie. Looking professional is key and solid dark colors usually portray a more professional appearance. It is respectful and still expected that you dress better than those who may be interviewing you.

In the medical field if scrubs are normal interview attire, make sure they are clean and pressed. In all cases, shoes should be clean, closed toe and low heeled, in case you are asked to take a tour which requires a lot of walking. Casual, skimpy and sloppy attire is NOT acceptable. Also, do not wear a lot of jewelry or strong perfume or cologne as this detracts from you the person and your qualifications. It is also a best practice to minimize visible body art and piercings during interviews because you do not know how the interviewer will perceive them and it may be distracting. The night before take 15 minutes to review your suit or outfit and your shoes, and make sure that everything is clean, pressed and in good shape. If in doubt, consult with a trusted advisor on your attire.

6. **When you arrive at the Interview Location turn your PHONE OFF** – (not vibrate) or better yet DON'T BRING IT or LEAVE IT IN THE CAR to ensure you portray a positive, interested professional demeanor at all times.

   Why? Think about how often you pick up and view your phone screen, afraid you will miss a call or text. Viewing your phone screen during and between interviews, as well as while you are waiting in a conference room, in an office, in the lobby or in the restroom between interviews will be seen by someone in the company and may be viewed by a potential employer as non interest in the job. In fact, they may even wonder how much you might be distracted by your personal device versus completing actual work for them, if they hired you.

7. **Rehearse your body language** – First impressions are made within the first 10 seconds of meeting someone so practice ahead of time to make them count. In those 10 seconds they will observe your behavior, in terms of how you walk in the room, whether you stand up when someone new enters or leaves the room, whether you look them in the eye

(if culturally acceptable), provide a firm hand shake or other accepted greeting, introduce yourself and SMILE!

Practice all of these actions. If you have a trusted audience (a significant other, a family member, a friend), run through your greeting routine. Have the other person ask you a few mock interview questions, and ask them to note any posture or demeanor issues. Try to engage them in some general small talk to get you ready for that as well.

Even if you don't have a trusted audience, you can still prepare using a mirror or better yet, the recording device on one of your electronics. Practice your easy interview smile and your "ask me about my accomplishments" sitting posture. Believe it or not, just putting some thought into where you put your hands or how you cross or place your legs and feet can help keep you calm and feel more at ease during the interview.

This is particularly important if you are shy or have trouble speaking. Conducting mock interviews with a trusted advisor, responding out loud in front of mirror and recording yourself will ensure your success. Another long-term tactic to consider is joining a Toastmasters chapter or acting class in your area to continue increasing your comfort level speaking in front of an audience.

8. **Rehearse your talking points and answers to potential questions** – While the interviewer is going to have your resume in front of them, neither of you will be interested in running verbatim through the document. In the next section we will explore the best ways to develop specific, real-world examples

covering the points in your resume so you are prepared to talk about them.

From a general standpoint, it is important to remember that you are how you speak and act, so communicating clearly using correct pronunciation and grammar will be important. You should never answer a question with just a 'yes' or 'no,' instead prepare examples to elaborate, for example, "Yes, I (took this action) to resolve (this issue) which resulted in (this outcome)."

It is important to be yourself, however, do not use any slang or acronyms in your speech, and minimize personal details about your life to avoid possible inaccurate assumptions by the interviewer.

Actions you want to avoid include these types of behaviors which studies indicate are the primary reason a candidate is NOT hired:

- Poor personal appearance
- Inability to communicate clearly
- Poor voice and grammar
- No career plan – no purpose/goals
- Lack of enthusiasm & confidence
- Failure to look the interviewer in the eye (if culturally acceptable)
- Limp hand shake
- Late to the interview
- Does not thank the interviewer for their time
- Asks no questions
- Lack of knowledge about company or position
- Condemning past employers

Always listening attentively while sitting or standing quietly and responding with a thoughtful, professional response will ensure your success.

Interview Preparation is the Key to Success

Interviewing today is a combination of Traditional Interview Questions, such as 'Tell me about yourself' and Behavioral Interview Questions, such as, "Describe a situation in which you used good judgment and logic in solving a problem," which are intended to elicit detailed responses from the candidate. The goal of these questions is to determine if you possess the desired Soft Skill characteristics necessary for the job, such as, critical thinking, being a self-starter, willingness to learn, willingness to travel, self-confidence, teamwork or professionalism.

Traditional Interview Questions

Traditional interview questions are still asked, almost as a default to open an interview. *"Tell me about yourself"* is a standard. For those entering a career change, the interviewer may ask, *"What made you decide to go to school to become a (new degree major, ex. pharmacy technician)."* To cover uncomfortable pauses during the interview, you may be asked *"What do you like or dislike about working in customer service (or other type of job function)?"* Therefore, it is very important to prepare ahead of time. Since these are usually the three most frequently asked questions, here are some guidelines to think about when framing your response:

Interview Opening: Tell me about yourself

Based on all your research about this company and the job description of the position you are applying for, think about what the interviewer may be looking for. It could be your commitment to the area where the company is located; commitment to staying in a job long-term; a specific reason why you are interested in this company or industry or some other factors which are important to the interviewer. It is NOT about sharing personal details about your family members, problems you may have at home or in past jobs or your life story.

Not a good response:

Well, I have 2 children, 5 & 10 at home and now that my youngest is going to kindergarten in the fall, I'm looking for job to get out of the house.

As an interviewer, my immediate thought is that "Oh no, she's going to have day care problems, trouble getting to work on time or calling to say she will not be in, because she has to stay home with a sick child," all because the candidate has put her family first in this response. And unbeknownst to you, the interviewers feeling may be compounded because the last person who had this job had similar challenges. Guess what, this response will ultimately put this candidate in the 'no' pile.

Good responses:

I will complete my xx degree at (university name) in April and am looking for a (job name) position with a company, such as yours who values a hardworking, detail oriented, dedicated employee with extensive customer service experience.

I recently relocated to (city name) for my spouse's employment and looking for a management opportunity in the xx field, which utilizes my expertise in cost estimating, accounting, etc. My research on (Company name you're interviewing for) indicates it is a great place to work and I thank you for the opportunity to further explore the (position name applying for) in more detail.

My background is in business management and following a brief caregiving respite, which has now been resolved, I am looking for a new opportunity in (city name) where I have relocated. My research on (Company name you're interviewing for) indicates it is a great place to work and I thank you for the opportunity to further explore the (position name applying for) in more detail.

As an interviewer, I can relate to all three examples, which portray a candidate who has done their homework about my company, is confident, hardworking and knowledgeable about the field and position and is likely to remain in the area long-term for the correct opportunity. In this case, this candidate goes into the short 'yes' pile.

Career Change Question

Practice your response to this question so it comes out smoothly and with enthusiasm. There is usually a specific reason you picked a new career path, so share that with the interviewer so they know you are truly interested in this career path and plan to stick with it. The following example refers to the resume in Appendix 7.

Q: You have a lot of experience in different fields, what made you decide to become a pharmacy technician?

> *After graduating with my BA and working as an office manager, I realized I was interested in moving into the medical field. I had enjoyed my time working in retail at (Drug Store Name), as well as volunteering at the Humane society, so I researched degrees which utilized my expertise and interest in customer service and business within the medical field and decided to follow this path. My internship last year solidified my decision, as I found it very rewarding. In fact, long term I would like to become a Pharmacist.*

In this response, the candidate has given a believable reason for this big change in their career, incorporating other aspects of their work experience from their resume, showing commitment through education completion and stating long term aspirations to stay in this field.

Like/Dislike Questions:

These should be answered in a similar professional vein, focused on Soft Skill attributes the interviewer is looking for in the job description or what you uncover throughout the interview. You can use Behavioral Interview responses as part of your answer. This is particularly important for the Dislike question, because it gives you an opportunity to turn it around into a positive. Using the resume in Appendix 7, for example,

> *While, not really a dislike I have found that customer service can be difficult when a customer gets frustrated and angry. (As I outlined in my previous example), my approach of staying calm, listening carefully and restating the issue back to them, followed by an action plan to resolve this issue usually ends well and ensures all parties, myself included are satisfied. (In that example, Mr Smith ended very happy with the resolution and even gave the company a good online review)*

In the above example this response is strongest when a specific situation you have already shared during the interview or a new example is incorporated as part of the response. Overall, the response demonstrates you know how to handle a "dislike" emotion professionally and you are focused on the customer, while remaining calm and cool under pressure. In this case, this allows the candidate to remain in the short 'yes' pile.

Now let's move on to Behavioral Interview questions.

Behavioral Interview Questions

The premise behind behavioral interviewing questions is that the most accurate predictor of future performance is past performance in similar situations. Behavioral interviewing, in fact, is said to be 55 percent predictive of future on-the-job behavior, while traditional interviewing is only 10 percent predictive. Behavioral Interview Questions allow employers to evaluate a candidate's past experiences and behaviors so they can determine the applicant's potential for success.

Before the interviewing process begins, the interviewer will identify specific job-related experiences, behaviors, knowledge, skills and abilities that the company has decided are desirable for the position you are interviewing for. Then the employer uses this information to structure very pointed questions to elicit detailed responses aimed at determining if the candidate possesses the desired characteristics, such as, critical thinking, being a self-starter, willingness to learn, willingness to travel, self-confidence, teamwork and professionalism.

Typical questions start out: "Tell about a time..." or "Describe a situation..." related to the type of skill they are enquiring about. It is a formal interviewing methodology. Interviewers are asked to record the candidate's responses and after the interview provide a rating in order to evaluate candidates selected criteria during the interview. That is why, in this situation, you will often see the interviewer with their head down, scribbling furiously on their form. In fact, often these types of interviews are conducted in groups, where, for example, 3 employees interview the candidate around a table at the same time. This format is designed to allow them to capture all the information the candidate shares and still observe your non-verbal behaviors.

How Candidates Should Respond to Behavioral Interview Questions

Ideally, when asked a situational question it is best to use a three step process, where
1. You briefly describe a situation,
2. You describe what specific action you took which had an effect on the situation, and
3. You outline the situation result or outcome.

Think about it as framing your response as a three-step process, usually called a S-A-R, P-A-R, or S-T-A-R statement.
1. Situation (or task, problem)
2. Action (you took)
3. Result/outcome

Your response, using this three step process is what the interviewers have been asked to record on their paperwork, so be sure to cover all three parts in each of your responses. It is important to note that in step 2 you need to be sure to describe the specific actions <u>you, yourself</u> took in the situation, and in step 3 there does not always need to be a positive outcome. Sometimes the outcome is a follow up to next steps or it is a compromise all parties agreed to abide by. The key here is your answer in step 3 indicates that an effective closure for all parties was reached.

A list of common categories and questions is listed in **Appendix 10**. Typically these questions are asked so you can demonstrate your actions related to specific points on your resume.

Example

For demonstration purposes, I will use the Pharmacy Technician resume in **Appendix 7** and in the responses below, will break my answer out into the 3 steps so the flow is evident.

Let's use the following position description which I found on an online job board as an example of desired Soft Skills attributes desired: *"Candidate must be detail oriented, able to complete basic math functions, and have some computer skills. The individual must also exemplify exceptional customer service, demonstrate a consistent long standing work history, have a willingness to learn and commitment to achieving goals set by management."*

Based on this job description, we can assume that the behavioral question categories listed below will be included in the interview. Therefore, before the interview the candidate should prepare a response to a sample question in each category by referencing the bullet points in different parts of their resume to reinforce their qualifications for the job. Then the candidate should practice these responses "out loud" so it doesn't sound rehearsed. Of course, the key to success is to decide which examples from your resume you will use to best demonstrate you are the best candidate for the job.

Behavioral Interviewing Categories and Questions

Decision Making and Problem Solving

Describe a situation in which you used good judgment and logic in solving a problem.

1. While working at the Drug Store as a customer service associate, a customer stopped me in the aisle to ask about some senior products for themselves. They were somewhat embarrassed, but struggling with the decision, and I found out later they had limited income and mobility, 2. I quietly asked them a few questions, and directed them to the correct shelf, where we reviewed sizes and brands. The customer was still concerned, so 3. I offered to walk to the back of the store and ask the pharmacists opinion while she is waiting in the aisle for me. She was very grateful for my assistance and left the store satisfied.

Related to the resume in Appendix 7 this response demonstrates the soft skills desired of exceptional customer service as well as good judgement and logic to solve a problem.

Communication

Q – Describe a situation in which you were able to successfully communicate with another individual who did not personally like you (or vice versa).

1. One of the managers at the fast food restaurant I worked at was very strict with regards to following rules and procedures. One of those was ensuring customers' orders were filled accurately, with little waste in a timely manner. The stores were actually graded on things like this by the corporate office. 2. I made a point of clearly understanding the manager's priorities and ensuring they were met. In the case of customer order accuracy, I suggested and we added a quick extra check step which was easy for everyone to understand and implement. 3. As a result, I received a promotion to cashier and before leaving, was a closing supervisor.

Related to the resume in Appendix 7 this response demonstrates the soft skills desired of having a willingness to learn and commitment to achieving goals set by management, exceptional customer service as well as the ability to communicate effectively with everyone.

Interpersonal Skills

Q – Give me an example of what you have done in the past to contribute to a teamwork environment.

1. While working at Jewelry Brokers most of my time was spent arranging displays, updating marketing materials and other back room duties, however, 2. often we were short staffed on the floor when sales associates were busy or unable to answer the telephone. They were commission based, while I was not. However, I was knowledgeable of the merchandise and wanted to make sure our customers' needs were met, so I worked out a method where the sales associates could make an introduction and handoff to me, when busy, for follow up and to meet their needs, 3. thus ensuring our customers' needs were met in a timely manner and the sales associates received their commissions.

Related to the resume in Appendix 7, this response demonstrates the soft skills desired of exceptional teamwork and customer service and taking the initiative to solve a problem. The two-year work history listed in the resume also implies a consistent long standing work history.

Planning and Organization

Q – Describe how you've handled a sudden interruption to your schedule.

As you know working retail, interruptions are the norm. 1. While working as a Pharmacy Technician Intern, I was restocking shelves and removing out of date product when a customer at the pharmacy counter fell down in what appeared to be a medical emergency. 2. I quickly went to their assistance and after briefly assessing the situation, asked for the Pharmacist assistance. I then called 911 and they were transported to the hospital. 3. Luckily it was not a busy time of day. After they departed, I cleaned up the customer waiting area for the Pharmacist and returned to my stocking duties. The scanning equipment assisted me in identifying where I had stopped, so minimal overlap of work was required.

Related to the resume in Appendix 7 this response demonstrates the soft skills desired traits of detail orientation; ability to work effectively under pressure to organize the solve to an urgent problem and compassion. Exceptional customer care is also evident.

Motivation

Q – Tell me about a time when you went above and beyond the call of duty.

1. While volunteering at the Humane Society we had a call of an injured dog about 5 miles from the kennel. 2. I offered to go pick it up and bring it back for the kennel medical staff to take care of. 3. I then also provided foster care while he recovered until he was adopted.

Related to the resume in Appendix 7 this response uses one of the two volunteer activities listed and demonstrates the soft skills of compassion, willingness to go above and beyond the call of duty as well as the ability to work effectively long term under pressure to solve an urgent problem.

It should be noted that expertise and experience listed the Skills and Volunteer Experience sections of the resume in Appendix 7 imply the soft skills of being able to complete basic math functions, detail orientation and computer skills, which may lead to additional questions in these areas. While this candidate may be involved in other volunteer activities, these sections should only include information relevant to the job search.

There are two other areas of Interviewing questions that are important to cover, which include how to answer difficult or illegal questions and how to close an interview.

How to protect your right to privacy without jeopardizing a job offer

It is a fact of life. Not everyone is trained on how to interview effectively, and some think they know it all. As a result you need to be prepared when an interviewer asks those difficult and sometimes illegal questions. Again, preparation and practicing your responses "out loud" is the key.

The secret of replying to questions that intrude on your rights to privacy, or even those that fall into a "gray" area, is to relate your answers to job performance. You basically have 3 choices.

- You can refuse to answer, and tell the employer you think the question is improper.
- You can swallow your pride and your privacy and answer the question as asked.
- You can answer the legitimate concern that probably lies behind the wrongful question and ignore the improper question itself – the best of both worlds.

They may feel justified in asking some of these questions, based on past employee behavior which they are looking to avoid, or for some other reason, and they might get mad if you don't answer, but that does not make it right. Below are some examples of questions and how you might respond. At the end of the day, you will need decide if this type of behavior is acceptable from a potential employer, and if not, move on.

Q & A Examples

Q: Do you plan to have children? A: *I plan to pursue a career whether or not I decide to raise a family.*

Q: Are you aware that we've usually hired a more athletic person for this job because the pressure and fatigue of a lot of travel? (Read: someone not overweight.) A: *There's no task in your job description that I can't perform.*

Q: What's your general state of health? A: *I'll be glad to take a pre-employment exam by your company physician to be sure I'm able to handle the job.*

Q: Is your spouse employed? A: *Yes, and very supportive of my seeking employment here.*

Q: Have you ever been arrested other than for traffic violations? A: *There's nothing I've ever done that would give your company any concern that I'd breach any trust that the job you have requires.*

Q: Do you own your own home, rent or live with your parents? A: *I'm not sure how this relates to the job. Can you explain?*

Be aware of end runs, particularly on age. The interviewer says, "Oh, I see that you attended Cornell. What years were you there?" The plain fact is that of all questions an employer might ask, the most publicized "no-no" is age. A good response, to avoid offending the interviewer with this query may be *"Did someone else here graduate from there, too?"* That answer will divert the interviewer from the subject and get the discussion back on track.

When all else fails, feel free to fall back on the response: *I'm not sure how this relates to the job. Can you explain?*

Always Prepare Questions to Ask the Interviewer

You must ask a least one question, usually toward the end of the interview, or you signal lack of interest in the job or opportunity. DO NOT ask about the company insurance plan or salary. These points are typically discussed, once a job offer has been made. Rather focus on questions which allow you to reiterate your fit for the job and company.

Examples of questions you might ask at a job interview:

Can you describe a typical day for someone in this position? or What is the top priority of the person who accepts this job?

How will my leadership responsibilities and performance be measured? And by whom?

How often?

Can you describe the company's management style or corporate culture?

Does the organization support ongoing training and education for employees to stay current in their fields?

Why did you come to work here? What keeps you here?

What are the traits and skills of people who are the most successful within the organization?

Following each response from the interviewer, use the opportunity to reiterate why you are a good fit. Never ask about salary and benefit issues until those subjects are raised by the employer.

Strategies to Close the Interview "Sale" Effectively

After you have asked your questions at the end of the interview, be prepared to leave your interviewer with the right picture of you.

- Think of at least five skills or traits you want remembered after the interview. Choose something "concrete." When you answer with, "I have great communication skills, and I am a hard worker," you will not stand out.

Example: *"I have two skills that are distinctly different but that define my personality. I am a very good pianist and an excellent 'computer guy.' I'm known for my love of keyboards."*

- Ask if there is anything else you can provide. Examples include references, transcripts, background information, and samples.

  Example: *"Is there any other information that I can provide that would convince you that I am the right person for this job?"*

- State your interest in the position, sound interested and tell what added value you can bring to the job.

  Example: *"From what you have been telling me about this position, and from what I know about your company, I know that I have the right mix of experience and education to bring value to this position. Based on past experiences I can 'ramp up' quickly and be on board with projects within the first few weeks."*

- Ask about the next step in the process.

- It's important for you to know the next step for follow up. Ask for the decision date, if possible.

  Example: *"I'm interested in knowing what the next step in the process is and when you will be making a decision so I can follow up."*

- Find out how to contact the interviewer. If you don't hear back, you will need to know whom to contact and whether the employer will accept calls to check the status.

  Example: *"I'd like to stay in touch and follow up with you in a week or two to see how the process is going and where I*

*stand. How do you prefer that I communicate with you —
email or phone?"*

Closing the sale is important. So tailor your questions to
the position you are interviewing for.

Remember... You Will Be Rated After the Interview on
the Following Attributes:
40% Attitude
5% Communication Skills
25% Appearance
10% Job Qualifications

It goes back to what employers are looking for and will
be saying as they meet to decide who to bring back or
make an offer to. If you have the right educational or
work background, they know they can train you. So iden-
tifying which of the following attributes are important to
the employer, which you will find out through your re-
search and interview skills become critically important:
Attitude over aptitude
Positive and Outgoing
Honest
Eager to learn
On time
Flexible
Dependable
Knowledgeable
Professional Confident
Compassion
Organized
Loyal

Now that I have shared the basics I encourage you to PRACTICE, A LOT!

In Appendix 11-14 I have provided four example interviewing guides to use when conducting practice Mock Interviews

Appendix 15 includes a Mock Interview Evaluation sheet to be completed by the Mock Interviewer.

To use these tools effectively, follow these steps:
1. Beforehand, identify and practice example responses to each question based on your resume which you plan to use in an interview.
2. Find one or more trusted friends to be your Mock Interviewer(s).
3. Agree to meet your Mock Interviewer in a room with a table or desk so you can sit across from each other.
4. Once they are seated, you, as the interviewee leave the room.
5. To Practice your Body Language, you enter the room and practice your professional greeting, before being seated.
6. To Practice your Talking Points and Answers, the Interviewer will ask and record your responses using one of the Mock Interviewing Guides. Plan for the interview to last 30 minutes.
7. The Interviewer then asks you if you have any questions, and provides made up responses.
8. When the Interviewer closes the Mock Interview, you, as the Interviewee provide a professional closing and leave the room.

9. The Interviewer then fills out the Mock Interview Evaluation Guide related to both your verbal and nonverbal behavior found in Appendix 15 and shares that data with you.

There are 4 different Mock Interview guides provided in Appendix 11-14 so you have plenty of opportunities to practice. Think about using multiple mock interviewers over time to get used to a variety of interviewing styles. *Remember, the more prepared and practiced you are, the more relaxed and confident you will be during the real interviews. Believe me, it will show!*

In Closing...

Remember: Finding a Job is a Roller Coaster Ride with High High's and Low Low's.

If you don't get this job, and all a potential employer can say is 'No," then learn from your mistakes and move on to another. If you take at least one of the following actions EVERY SINGLE DAY until you find a job, you will be successful.

- Network/Request an Informational Interview
- Follow Up. Follow Up. Follow Up until you get a 'No'
- Join and become actively involved in associations, clubs, volunteer
- Set alerts for new job listings
- Continue building your professional online presence by liking, sharing or post content relevant to your industry or local job market

- Post your resume copy in your professional online profile, adding updates as they occur
- Research for additional opportunities
- Send your resume to one company
- Send another Thank You Note & ask for "who else they recommend you talk to about your career aspirations"
- Email a network or reference contact to update them on your search and share a piece of content that may be of interest to them
- Find a coach to keep you pumped and practice interview questions with
- Constantly network
- **Stay Positive. Don't give Up... You will get hired!**

Even after you're hired, I encourage you to continue networking and periodically update your resume on line and on paper to make this process less painful the next time... and there will be a next time, guaranteed!

NETWORKING & INFORMATIONAL INTERVIEW QUESTIONS YOU CAN ASK

There is no need to memorize these questions. Just start off with the 3 or 4 you like the most. Master them and then give the others a test run.

How did you get involved in...?
- *What made you decide to major in...?*
- *What made you decide to attend (name of school)?*
- *What made you decide to go into the ____business?*
- *How did you get your start in the ____ business?*

What advice would you give me if I wanted to be successful in your line of work (or major)?
- *What advice would you give someone just starting in this business/profession/major?*

What do you love/enjoy most about what you do?

- *What do you love/enjoy most about your business/profession/major?*

What separates you from the competition?

- *What separates your business/company/organization from the competition?*
- *What separates your school from other schools like it?*

What one thing would you do if you knew that you could not fail?

- *What one thing would you do with your business if you knew that you could not fail?*
- *What one thing would you do if you knew you were guaranteed to succeed?*

What was the strangest or funniest incident you've experienced in your business?

- *What was the strangest or funniest incident you've experienced at your school?*
- *What was the strangest or funniest incident you've experienced in your organization?*

What significant changes have you seen take place in your profession/area of expertise through the years?

- *What significant changes have you seen take place at your school since you've been here?*
- *What significant changes have you seen take place in your major since you chose it?*

What do you see as the coming trends in your profession/area of expertise?

- *How do think your school will be different in the future?*
- *What do you see as the coming trends in your major?*
- *What do you think will change about your major in the future?*

So, (person's name), if someone were to describe you in one sentence what would she say?

- *If someone were to describe your business/company/school in one sentence what would he say?*
- *What ways have you found to be the most effective for promoting your business/ organization/product?*

It's the end of a great week and you have some free time on your hands – what would you do?

- *What do you like to do in your spare time?*

What would make someone the ideal employee for your company or organization?

- *How would you describe the ideal client/customer/prospect/employee for your company/organization?*
- *What would make someone a perfect fit for your profession/major/school/company/ organization?*

Key To Success

Show you are truly interested in the other person. Be interested, ask questions, and let the other person do the talking

APPENDIX 2

THANK YOU LETTER EXAMPLES

Good afternoon (name),

Thank you for taking the time to speak with me yesterday about the (position name) position with xx company. It was a pleasure meeting with you, and I truly enjoyed learning more about the role and the company.

After our conversation, I am confident that my skills and experiences are a great match for this opportunity. As we discussed, I believe my background in xx and xx skills and my ability to manage (a process or task discussed) will serve me well in meeting the needs of your customers.

I am very enthusiastic about the possibility of joining the (xx company) team and would greatly appreciate a follow-up as you move forward with the hiring process. If you need any further information, please do not hesitate to contact me by email or phone. Thanks again, and I hope to hear from you in the near future.

Best regards,

Dear *Mr./Ms. Last Name:*

Thank you very much for the opportunity to interview for the position of *[job title]* yesterday *[or today, if appropriate]*. I enjoyed speaking with you, meeting other members of the staff, and the opportunity to learn more about this position. I am very interested in this position and the opportunity to join your team.

This job feels like a very good match between my skills and experience and the requirements of this job. As we discussed, you need someone with strong *[whatever]* skills, and I have extensive experience with *[whatever technology or tool that is important to the job and that you have experience using]*. In addition, in my current *[or former]* job as *[names or type of employer in your past]* has provided the opportunity to polish my skills in*[whatever]* and *[whatever]* needed for your *[job title]* position.

Again, thank you for considering me for this wonderful opportunity. Please let me know if you have any questions or concerns or need more information. I look forward to hearing from you next week *[or whenever they said they would be in touch]* and hope to join your staff soon.

Best regards,

If you interviewed with multiple people, personalize a little differently for each one based on what you talked about in the interview, in case they compare their letters.

CHANGING CAREER, CLINICAL EXPERIENCE VS OTHER WORK EXPERIENCE

(Your Name)

Street address, City, State, Zipcode
(xxx) xxx-xxxx
Email address

OBJECTIVE

Seeking an entry-level diagnostic medical sonography position, focused on providing compassionate patient care, excellent communication skills and quality diagnostic imaging.

EDUCATION

University Name, City, State   Expected graduation:
April 201x

Associates of Science in Diagnostic Medical Sonography
- ARDMS Sonography Principles and Instrumentation completed April 2016
- Certified CPR, HIPPA, OSHA, BBP/HIV

College Name, City, State
- Completed Medical Assisting Certification

CLINICAL EXPERIENCE   201x

Hospital Name, City, State   December 2016
                                              February 2017

Clinical Student

- Proficient in Vascular and Invasive Procedures, as well as Abdomen and GYN ultrasound imaging
- Performed patient care tasks as assigned
- Completed assigned proficiencies

Community Health Center Name, City, State   October –
                                              November 2016

Clinical Student

- Proficient in Abdomen, Vascular and Small Parts ultrasound imaging
- Responsible for maintaining a clean and sterile patient rooms
- Completed additional clinical duties, as needed

WORK EXPERIENCE

Medical Clinic Name, City, State   2011-2014

Physical Therapist Technician

- Assisted patients with physical movements to help restore function and lessen pain and disability.
- Instructed patients in the safe and effective use of pulleys, weights, inclined surfaces and other equipment.
- Administered massage and well as heat, water, ice, electrical, and light stimulation as part of therapeutic programs.

Restaurant Name, City, State   2013

Hostess

- Greeted and seated customers with a positive and friendly attitude
- Accurately scheduled online and telephone reservations each day

PAST MILITARY; EDUCATED, CHANGING CAREER

First, Last Name

Street address, City, State, Zipcode xxx.xxx.xxxx firstlast name@gmail.com

Objective

An entry-level sonography position within an organization seeking an organized team player, quality diagnostic imaging, and compassionate patient care.

Education and Training

(Name) University | Fort Myers, FL   *xxxx-Present*

Associates of Science in Diagnostic Medical Sonography

- Expected graduation: December 2015
- ARDMS Sonography Principles and Instrumentation passed 12/13/14
- Member of Phi Theta Kappa Honor Society
- Honor Roll: 3.5 GPA
- Certified CPR, HIPAA, BBP/OSHA

Community College of the Air Force | *City, State*
Associates of Science in Weather Technology

- 97 Credit Hours completed during military training

Clinical & Professional Experience *xxxx-xxxx*

Company Name, City, State *xxxx-xxxx*
Clinical Student

- Experience with Acuson Sequoia 512 LCD, Acuson Antares
- Proficient in Patient Care, OBGYN, and Vascular ultrasound imaging

Company Name, City, State *xxxx-xxxx*
Clinical Student

- Experience with Acuson Sequoia 512 LCD
- Proficient in Patient Care, Abdomen, and Vascular ultrasound imaging

Company Name, City, State *xxxx-xxxx*
Patient Access Specialist I

- Schedule and confirm patient diagnostic appointments, surgeries, and medical consultations
- Receive and route messages or documents, such as laboratory results, to appropriate staff

United States Air Force, City, State *xxxx-xxxx*
Meteorologist

- Air Force Accommodation Medal Recipient
- Formulate predictions by interpreting environmental data
- Provide aircrews with forecast and observations needed for airfield management and flight planning

EXPERIENCED, MILITARY CAREER CHANGE

Your Name

Address phone number
City, state, zip code
email

OBJECTIVE

A Medical Billing and Coding position in the (City) (State), which utilizes my recent degree and extensive work experience in customer service, budgeting, accounting, inventory control, MS Word and industry specific software.

EDUCATION

Medical Billing & Coding Certificate, Cape Coral Tech   May 201x

Military Quartermaster Courses, US Army, completed 84 credit hours   xxxx

WORK EXPERIENCE

Manager, company name, city, state   xxxx-xxxx

- Lead manager of a high volume fast food restaurant including hiring and managing staff, inventory, payroll, cash control, customer service and ensured all food safety procedures were followed
- Successfully implemented training procedures to handle customer fluctuations and emergency procedures

- Hired and trained all employees and established a process for seasonal and community events to grow sales

General Manager, company name, city, state   xxxx-xxxx
- Lead manager of a high volume fast food restaurant including hiring and managing staff, inventory, payroll, cash control, customer service and ensured all food safety procedures were followed
- Successfully increased sales year over year and consistently passed state and corporate inspections
- Responsible for all incoming new manager training

Services Supervisor, company name, city, state   xxxx-xxxx
- Responsible for customer service, supervising staff, all maintenance and ordering and managing inventory
- Successfully lead refurbishment of all guest rooms and reorganized a computer inventory system which integrated all lodging functions.

Area Manager, Army & Air Force Exchange   xxxx-xxxx
Service, city, state
- Promoted from various clerical and supervisory positions to manage a Home & Garden Center with $3.5mm in sales
- Successfully managed 15 employees directly and was responsible for managing 90 employees as closing manager
- Responsible for maintaining the RPOS 3 computer system for daily receipts and the inventory for 3 departments
- Successfully coordinated the construction and opening of a new Home and Garden Center

Material Control & Accounting Specialist, United   xxxx-xxxx
States Army
- **Manager Tech Supply Unit**
  - Promoted to manage 14 Tech Supply Units providing maintenance and support of military vehicles and aircraft

- o Successfully trained and supervised employees on new computer systems
- o Experienced in conducting warehouse inspections and investigated inventory discrepancies
- o Assisted in a downsizing consolidation of 14 units into 7 units
- **Parts Clerk**
  - o Successfully maintained inventory for 300 products lines and bench stock of 1000 items to repair technical vehicles and systems crucial to defense

CERTIFICATIONS

- HIPPA Certified
- Basic Life Support
- Dale Carnegie Training

NEW CAREER, LIMITED WORK EXPERIENCE

Your Name
Address
Contact information

Objective
A Medical Billing and Coding position in the (City) (State), which utilizes my recent degree and work experience in customer service, budgeting, inventory control, MS Word and industry specific software.

Skills & Abilities
- Microsoft Office 2013 (Certified Word and Excel)
- Microsoft Office 2013 PowerPoint, Outlook, Access
- Experienced with Medisoft and medical terminology
- Index and Electronic filing
- Medical Office Administration

Experience
OUTPATIENT REGISTRATION VOLUNTEER LEE MEMORIAL HOSPITAL, FT. MYERS, FL 33901   xxxx –present
- Welcome patients

- Efficiently retrieve patient's medical record from file
- Successfully distribute medical records to get patient registered
- Assist patient to testing site

VOLUNTEER   xxxx – xxxx
Church Organization Name,
City, State, Zip

- Successfully organized, and managed a children's program, including teaching one of the classes
- Created and effectively executed a yearly calendar of events for all classes
- Ordered supplies needed for events, awards, etc. within budget

ASSISTANT MANAGER   xxxx – xxxx
GOODWILL STORE,
city, state, zip

- Inventoried and priced donated items to maximize profits
- Provided excellent customer satisfaction, often exceeding expectations
- Effectively and efficiently handled daily profits and bank deposits

Education   **Cape Coral Institute of Technology,** Cape Coral, FL 33993
Medical Administrative
Specialist Certification   Completed xxxx

CAREER CHANGE; MUCH EXPERIENCE IN DIFFERENT FIELDS

(Your Name)

xxxx ABC Street Cell: (xxx) xxx-xxxx
City, State, zip code Email Address.com

OBJECTIVE

An entry level pharmacy technician position within an organization seeking an organized, hard-working, detail oriented, team player with extensive customer service experience

SKILLS

Computer software: MS Office (Microsoft Word, Excel, and Power-Point) & Photoshop for graphic design projects

EDUCATION

Cape Coral Technical College,
Cape Coral, FL   Expected Graduation
                                                 Date: May 20XX

Pharmacy Technician Program

- Florida Registered Pharmacy Technician License, expected completion May 20XX
- CPR & First Aid Certifications, completed 20XX & 20XX

Florida Gulf Coast University, Fort Myers, FL
Bachelor of Arts Graduate, Psychology Major 20XX

CLINICAL/INTERN EXPERIENCE

Grocery Store Name, City, State   20XX
Pharmacy Technician Intern

- Observed and assisted the pharmacy technician in the nonprescription areas of the department while under the pharmacist's supervision at all times
- Provided courteous and prompt customer service and a friendly atmosphere to customers
- Assisted the pharmacy technician restock over-the-counter shelves, removing out-of-date product, as instructed

WORK EXPERIENCE

Jewelry Brokers, Inc., City, State
Office Manager   20XX – 20XX
Provided excellent customer service to current and new clients

- Responsible for cataloguing and maintaining store inventory, including accurate record keeping
- Executed store sets and promotions throughout the year
- Designed and maintained company website and all marketing materials for upcoming sales and programs

Drug Store Name, City, State
Customer Service Associate   20XX – 20XX

- Provided customers with courteous, fair, friendly, and efficient checkout service
- Responsible for stocking shelves and seasonal displays
- Successfully resolved customer issues and answered questions to ensure a positive customer experience

Fast Food Restaurant Name, City, State   20XX – 20XX

Customer Service & Cashier

- Completed customer orders, operated cash register and managed cash and credit; tended to all exchanges and returns while providing strong customer service through active listening and problem solving skills

VOLUNTEER EXPERIENCE

Gulf Coast Humane Society, City, State   20XX – present
Volunteer

- Actively involved in the daily general care of the animals including walking/exercising, socializing, grooming and cleaning kennels, including in-home foster care, as needed

Computers to Crayons, City, State   20XX – 20XX
Volunteer

- Repaired hardware and upgraded software on used equipment for classroom reuse

EMAIL SUBJECT LINE: APPLICATION FOR THE OPEN SONOGRAPHER POSITION

Your Name
Address
City, state, zip code Email address

Date

[Recipient Name]
[Title]
[Company Name]
[Street Address] [City, ST ZIP Code]

Dear [Recipient Name]:

I am applying for the Sonographer position recently posted on the employment page on the hospital website. As requested, I have attached a copy of my job application and resume.

I am graduating from (University name) with an Associate's degree in Sonography in April 2017 and I believe my degree along with my clinical experience will make me a strong candidate for this position. As my resume indicates, my key strengths include time management skills, critical thinking, and compassionate patient care.

The Sonographer position sounds like an exciting opportunity and a good fit with my skills. I would welcome an opportunity discuss this opportunity with you further and can be reached by email or phone. Thank you for your time and consideration. I look forward to hearing from you about this opportunity.

Sincerely,

Your name

COVER LETTER EXAMPLES

Name
Address
City, State, Zip code
phone email

Date, 20xx

Hiring Manager name
Title
Company name
Address

Dear hiring manager name, **Applying to Ad**

I am interested in the xx position (# in ad, and where you saw position posted, if available) within your company. As requested, I have attached a copy of my job application and resume.

The opportunity presented in this listing is intriguing. I am graduating from (college) with a degree in (major) and I believe my degree along with my experience will make me a strong candidate for this position. The key strengths I possess for success in this position include (name 2-3 attributes that make you a good fit related to the job description).

The (position) sounds like an exciting opportunity and a good fit with my skills. I would welcome an opportunity to discuss my fit with your organization further and can be reached at email and phone. Thank you for your time and consideration. I look forward to speaking with you about this employment opportunity.

Sincerely, Your Name

Networking Referral Follow Up

As you suggested, I am forwarding my resume to you for consideration for a six-month intern/co-op position at xx company beginning xx (time frame).

I am beginning my x year at x college. My major is x, but my career goal of (describe) and I would welcome any kind of position in this field (describe fields).

My record of school work, employment and volunteer activities demonstrate attributes that make me a valuable employee.

Strong academic skills: Achieved a GPA of x and (list any honors received)

Reliability and work ethic: In all my employment and volunteer positions, I have maintained an excellent record of being on time, prepared and eager to take on new responsibilities

Deep interest in (whatever field is): In addition to volunteering at x location, I have also done x in this field.

I am available to speak with you at any time. Thank you for your consideration. I am enthusiastic about this position and believe I will make a valuable intern/co-op employee.

Sincerely, your name

Are you looking for an enthusiastic, hardworking person for your xx team? **Cold Call Cover Letter**

As a x major (graduating with a x degree in x time frame), I gained a thorough understanding of the concepts of xx, xx and xx (requirements of the position). My activities/achievements during college expanded on my classroom learning. For example, I had an opportunity to take a leadership role that demonstrated my ability to 'get things done' while working effectively with both students and administrators.

This position at x company is a good match for my qualifications. My background, professionalism and enthusiasm will make me an effective member of your team.

Sincerely, your name

BEHAVIORAL INTERVIEWING QUESTION EXAMPLES BY SOFT SKILL

Prepare your responses ahead of time
using your Resume and practice!

Decision Making and Problem Solving

- *Describe a situation in which you used good judgment and logic in solving a problem.*
- *Give me an example of a time when you had to be quick in coming to a decision.*

Leadership

- *Have you ever had trouble getting others to agree with your ideas? How did you deal with the situation, and were you successful?*
- *Describe the most challenging group from which you've had to gain cooperation.*

Motivation

- *Tell me about a time when you went above and beyond the call of duty.*

- *Give me an example of a situation in which you positively influenced the actions of others.*

Communication

- *Describe a situation in which you were able to successfully communicate with another individual who did not personally like you (or vice versa).*
- *Give me an example of a time you had to use written communication to convey an important argument or idea.*

Interpersonal Skills

- *Give me examples of what you've done in the past to contribute to a teamwork environment.*
- *Give an example of an unpopular decision you've made, what the result was, and how you managed it.*

Planning and Organization

- *When scheduling your time, what method do you use to decide which items are priorities?*
- *Describe how you've handled a sudden interruption to your schedule.*

INTERVIEW 1 – MOCK INTERVIEW QUESTIONS

1. **Ask at least <u>one</u> of the following <u>Traditional Interview Questions</u> to break the ice**

   Tell me about yourself

   This field seems to be a departure from your past experience, how/why did you decide to pursue it?

   What skills from your past experience do you bring to this field?

   I see you work(ed) at _____, what do/did you like about working there?

2. **Ask at least <u>two or more</u> of the following <u>Behavioral Interview Questions</u> and record responses to determine if they answered your question**

   Describe a situation in which you used good judgment and logic in solving a problem.

   Situation _____

   Action _____

   Situation _____

Describe a situation in which you were able to successfully communicate with another individual who did not personally like you (or vice versa).

Situation _____

Action _____

Situation _____

Give me examples of what you've done in the past to contribute to a teamwork environment.

Situation _____

Action _____

Situation _____

When scheduling your time, what method do you use to decide which items are priorities?

Situation _____

Action _____

Situation _____

Tell me about a recent situation in which you had to deal with a very upset customer or co-worker

Situation _____

Action _____

Situation _____

INTERVIEW 2 – MOCK INTERVIEW QUESTIONS

1. Ask at least <u>one</u> of the following <u>Traditional Interview Questions</u> to break the ice

   Tell me about yourself

   This field seems to be a departure from your past experience, how/why did you decide to pursue it?

   What skills from your past experience do you bring to this field?

   I see you work(ed) at _____, what do/did you like about working there?

2. Ask at least <u>two or more</u> of the following <u>Behavioral Interview Questions</u> and record responses to determine if they answered your question

Give me an example of a time when you had to be quick in coming to a decision.

Situation _____

Action _____

Situation _____

Describe the most challenging group from which you've had to gain cooperation and how you did it.

Situation _____

Action _____

Situation _____

Tell me about a time when you went above and beyond the call of duty.
Situation _____
Action _____
Situation _____

Give me an example of a time when something you tried to accomplish and failed/missed a goal/didn't measure up to expectations.
Situation _____
Action _____
Situation _____

Describe how you've handled a sudden interruption to your schedule.
Situation _____
Action _____
Situation _____

APPENDIX 13

INTERVIEW 3 – MOCK INTERVIEW QUESTIONS

1. **Ask at least <u>one</u> of the following <u>Traditional Interview Questions</u> to break the ice**

    Tell me about yourself

    This field seems to be a departure from your past experience, how/why did you decide to pursue it?

    What skills from your past experience do you bring to this field?

    I see you work(ed) at _____, what do/did you like about working there?

2. **Ask at least <u>two or more</u> of the following <u>Behavioral Interview Questions</u> and record responses to determine if they answered your question**

Describe a situation in which you were able to use persuasion to successfully convince someone to see things your way.

Situation _____

Action _____

Situation _____

Tell me about a recent situation in which you had to deal with a very upset customer or co-worker.

Situation _____

Action _____

Situation _____

Give me an example of a time when you set a goal and were able to meet or achieve it.

Situation _____

Action _____

Situation _____

Give me an example of a time when you used your fact-finding skills to solve a problem.

Situation _____

Action _____

Situation _____

What would you do if I came to you at 5:00 pm with something that had to be completed by the next morning and you had a 6:00 appointment that evening?

Situation _____

Action _____

Situation _____

INTERVIEW 4 – MOCK INTERVIEW QUESTIONS

1. **Ask at least <u>one</u> of the following <u>Traditional Interview Questions</u> to break the ice**

   Tell me about yourself

   This field seems to be a departure from your past experience, how/why did you decide to pursue it?

   What skills from your past experience do you bring to this field?

   I see you work(ed) at _____, what do/did you like about working there?

2. **Ask at least <u>two or more</u> of the following <u>Behavioral Interview Questions</u> and record responses to determine if they answered your question**

   Describe and instance when you had to think on your feet to extract yourself from a difficult situation

   Situation _____

   Action _____

   Situation _____

Would your boss describe you as a team player? If so, give me an example.

Situation _____

Action _____

Situation _____

Tell me about a time when you had too many things to do and you were required to prioritize your tasks.

Situation _____

Action _____

Situation _____

Describe a time when you anticipated potential problems and developed preventive measures.

Situation _____

Action _____

Situation _____

When faced with multiple tasks all coming due at the same time, how do you prioritize them and

Situation _____

Action _____

Situation _____

MOCK INTERVIEW EVALUATION

Interviewee Name: _____

Date _____

Interviewer Name: _____

Please rate the interviewee on a scale of 1 (lowest) to 5 (highest) in the following areas:

Nonverbal Behaviors   (circle one)

1. Dressed appropriately   1 2 3 4 5

2. Firmly shook hand of interviewer
    before and after   1 2 3 4 5

3. Maintained eye contact
    with interviewer   1 2 3 4 5

4. Maintained good posture   1 2 3 4 5

5. Did not fidget   1 2 3 4 5

Verbal Behaviors   (circle one)

1. Greeted interviewer by name   1 2 3 4 5

2. Listened closely to questions 1 2 3 4 5

3. Answered questions completely,
   yet briefly   1   2   3   4   5

4. Emphasized qualifications   1   2   3   4   5

5. Pointed out work related skills   1   2   3   4   5

6. Focused on strengths; avoided
   weaknesses   1   2   3   4   5

7. Demonstrated knowledge
   of the field   1   2   3   4   5

8. Stated career goal(s) and related
   it to position   1   2   3   4   5

9. Displayed enthusiasm   1   2   3   4   5

10. Acted in polite manner   1   2   3   4   5

11. Asked appropriate questions
    of the interviewer   1   2   3   4   5

12. Spoke clearly and at a
    reasonable volume   1   2   3   4   5

13. Avoided use of phrases such as
    "um" and "you know"   1   2   3   4   5

14. Thanked the interviewer   1   2   3   4   5

Additional Comments/Suggestions:

_____

_____

_____

_____

_____

ThePracticalLeader.com
PowerlinesPress.com
www.Youtube.com/ThePracticalLeader
https://www.facebook.com/thepracticalleader/

Videos are available free of charge on
my YouTube channels. Links are on each
of the websites above or go to
http://www.youtube.com/ThePracticalLeader.

Know someone who could benefit from
The Practical Leader? Share the link:
www.ThePracticalLeader.com